guinea pig

understanding and
caring for your pet

Written by
Dr Anne McBride BSc PhD Cert.Cons FRSA

guinea pigs

understanding and
caring for your pet

Written by
Dr Anne McBride BSc PhD Cert.Cons FRSA

Magnet & Steel Ltd

www.magnetsteel.com

Every reasonable care has been taken in the compilation of this publication. The Publisher and Author cannot accept liability for any loss, damage, injury or death resulting from the keeping of guinea pigs by user(s) of this publication, or from the use of any materials, equipment, methods or information recommended in this publication or from any errors or omissions that may be found in the text of this publication or that may occur at a future date, except as expressly provided by law.

No animals were harmed in the making of this book.

The 'he' pronoun is used throughout this book instead of the rather impersonal 'it', however no gender bias is intended.

Printed and bound in China.

ISBN: 978-1-907337-03-1
ISBN: 1-907337-03-2

Contents

Perfect pets

Guinea pigs have been popular as pets for many hundreds of years. Here are some of the reasons why:

- Guinea pigs rarely bite or scratch and, if treated gently, like to be petted by their owners.

- They are sociable and 'talkative'.

- Guinea pigs are not expensive to buy, and once you have purchased your initial equipment, they are relatively inexpensive to keep.

- Guinea pigs are hardy animals that can live outside in a hutch and attached run, as long as the hutch is kept warm and draught free.

- Guinea pigs can also live in the house, in a suitably sized cage with attached exercise area. They can spend some time roaming free in other safe areas of the house.

- Guinea pigs are most active in the daytime, whereas creatures such as hamsters and gerbils are active at night.

- Guinea pigs are medium sized and weigh between 500- 900 g (1- 2 lbs) and so are easier to handle than smaller creatures such as hamsters.

- Guinea pigs come in many different colours and coat types.

Some people are allergic to the fur of animals and may suffer health problems if a pet is kept in the house. Your doctor can test for this, and if you have a problem, you may still be able to keep your guinea pigs outside in a hutch with a run attached and enjoy watching them.

Special
requirements

Guinea pigs are delightful creatures, with their rounded bodies, and seemingly happy and chatty nature. But, like all animals, they have their own specific needs which you need to know about before buying your first guinea pigs. This is important so you can have a good relationship with your guinea pigs, and they can live long, healthy and happy lives.

- You will need to handle your guinea pigs gently, as they are easily frightened, especially when picked up. For this reason, young children, especially under the age of seven, should be supervised.

- You need to give your guinea pigs the right food to stay fit and healthy. Guinea pigs have a special requirement for vitamin C and for high fibre food.

- Long haired guinea pigs will need grooming every day.

- You will need to frequently clean out the guinea pigs' home.

- You need to provide a large, safe area where your guinea pigs can exercise every day outside their hutch or cage.

- You will need to make arrangements for someone to look after your guinea pigs if you go away on holiday.

- You will need to make a weekly check of your guinea pig's teeth and nails to ensure they are not overgrown.

- You should keep two guinea pigs together for companionship and commit to looking after them throughout their life, which may be 6 years.

What is a guinea pig?

Guinea pigs are members of the rodent family. This is the largest group of mammals, and contains over 2,000 different species of varying size and shape, including squirrels, the tiny harvest mouse, (which weighs around 7 g, less than a third of an ounce) and beaver.

The guinea pig's proper name is 'Cavia aperea f porcellus' or 'Cavy' for short, which indicates it belongs to the branch of the rodents known as the Caviomorpha. Some of its closer cousins in this group include the chinchilla and the capybara which is the world's largest rodent, weighing in at an impressive 65 kg (140 lb). The word rodent comes from the latin word 'rodere', to gnaw, and gnawing is one thing all rodents have in common. They gnaw to get their food and to make their homes, think of beaver dams for example.

Rodents have four big front teeth, the incisors that are evolved for gnawing. These sharp chisel-shaped teeth meet together like pincers and are very effective. They grow continually throughout the animal's life.

Guinea pigs come from the grasslands and lower slopes of the Andes Mountains in South America. They eat mostly grasses, herbs and meadow plants, a diet full of fibre. Indeed, like rabbits, they need large amounts of fibrous food such as grass and hay in their diet every day to remain healthy.

Guinea pigs live on the surface, and though they are poor climbers and do not dig, they will use rock crevices and even burrows of other animals as safe places. Guinea pigs are sociable and peaceable animals that naturally live in small groups of 5- 10, with 3- 4 males and several females and their young. They will rest together, groom each other and play together. They run and chase each other, sometimes leaping in the air, with all four feet off the ground, changing direction in mid jump, a behaviour known as 'popcorning'. Research has shown that guinea pigs need to be reared and kept with at least one other guinea pig for companion.

Rock Cavy pictured

Guinea pigs have a long pregnancy of over 60 days and their young are born well developed, looking like miniature adults. Baby guinea pigs are born furry with their eyes and ears open and a full set of those important teeth and they are able to eat grass within a few days of birth. Females can breed when they are only 2- 3 months old.

It is important to realise that guinea pigs are prey animals and are a major source of food for many meat eating predators. They are hunted by animals on the ground and from the air by birds. This has an affect on everything they do. It is why they are continually nervous and on the alert. Guinea pigs are very adept at spotting danger. They have excellent hearing and the position of their eyes means they can see above as well as behind them. They run away to safety at the first sign of any danger. It is because they live in the open, have many enemies, and rely on speed to escape that they have such well developed young, which can also run away from danger.

The human link

The guinea pigs' predators included people. Indeed, it is estimated that man first started to keep and domesticate the guinea pig some 6,000 years ago. Certainly the Incas were keeping them nearly 3,000 years ago, both for food and for sacrifice in religious ceremonies. Throughout the ages, guinea pigs have been kept rather like pets, allowed to run around the home, or kept in pens, while providing a reliable supply of meat. Indeed guinea pigs are still a staple source of meat for people in some parts of South America.

In the 15th Century the Spanish discovered and invaded South America and adopted the native people's habit of keeping guinea pigs as a source of fresh meat, as they were easy to keep on the ships on the long voyage back to Europe. Some were kept as pets and the fashion for keeping them spread quickly across Europe and the US. It immediately became a 'fancy' animal, as people started to breed for variations in coat colour and length.

The guinea pig has been a popular animal for laboratory studies – indeed we talk about being a 'guinea pig' when we are the first to try something, an 'experimental subject'. The origin of the name guinea pig is lost in the mists of time. The guinea part may be because when they were first brought to Britain they were sold for a guinea (£1.05 – substantial sum in those days). Alternatively it could come from the name of the South American country Guyana. The pig part may refer to the squeaking noises they make, which are similar to those of suckling pigs.

The guinea pig's world

Find out how a guinea pig functions and how it sees the world.

Nose

Guinea pigs rely on smell to identify each other, find the best food, to avoid poisonous plants and to detect the scent of a nearby predator. They can recognise other guinea pigs and different people just by scent.

Whiskers

These are sensitive and are used to help the guinea pig find its way in the dark and as a measure to decide whether it can fit through a space.

Mouth

The guinea pig uses its large tongue and sensitive lips to test if items can be eaten.

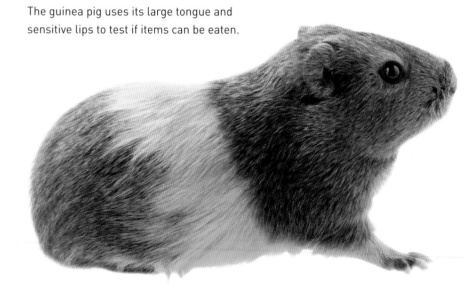

Teeth

The guinea pig's 20 teeth grow all the time – several inches a year. A constant supply of good quality hay and things for them to gnaw, such as untreated fruit tree or willow wood, is essential to prevent dental problems.

Eyes

Guinea pigs can see behind them, to the sides and above their head but not right in front of the nose, so approach them from the side so as to not startle them. They have excellent distance vision for movement, to help them detect predators, but do not see so well close up. They can see red, green and blue colours. Eyes can be red or black.

Ears

Like other rodents, guinea pigs can hear far better than we can. They can hear high pitched sounds which we cannot, in the ultra-sonic range. This means they hear noises from human equipment such as televisions and refrigerators. For guinea pigs these are very loud and stressful, and if you plan to keep your guinea pigs in the house you need to find somewhere quiet for them to live.

The ears are hairless, and, depending on the breed, can be small and upright – like the wild ancestor, large and rose shaped, or drooping.

Feet

The front feet have four claws (nails) and the back only three. The soles of the feet are bare.

Movement

Like us, guinea pigs walk on their heels. They walk, run and jump. When relaxed they have a shuffling gait with the body held close to the ground, when excited they will have a trotting gait holding their body high.

Tail

Guinea pigs have a tail but it is very short and is not visible on the outside of the body. An X-ray image would show the eight bones that make up the guinea pig's tail and these can be felt under the skin if you gently stroke your guinea pig's rump.

Body

The body is compact and rounded.

Coat

The coat may be short or long or even curly, fine or coarse. It may be a single colour, mixture or have special markings depending on the type of guinea pig. There are even hairless breeds!

Coat
varieties

The breeds and varieties of guinea pig available are distinguished by their coat colour and type. You may wish to have a particular variety, especially if you wish to show your guinea-pig. However, there are many crossbred guinea pigs which will have their own unique colouring and coat type and will also make excellent pets.

Colours & markings

Self pattern

All one colour. These are all smooth coated. Colours include white, cream, buff (a dark cream colour), gold, black, slate, lilac (a light grey shade), chocolate, beige and red (a mahogany reddish brown).

Marked pattern

More than one colour. Different varieties include:

Agouti

Like a wild guinea pig, with more than one colour on each strand of hair, creating a banded effect. The original colours were grey and brown, but you can get others such as silver agouti, or the Argentè, which has pink eyes and lilac or golden ticking on the coat.

Roan

Similar to the Agouti but the head and feet are solid black and the body is black with white hairs interspersed.

Brindle

Even mixture of black, brown and white hairs.

Silver

Dark coloured coat interspersed with silver hairs.

Bicolour

The coat is made up of blocks of two different colours.

Dutch

A particular type of bicolour where most of the body is of one colour, or is agouti, but there is a white saddle on the back and a white blaze on the face.

Dalmatian

Again two colours, but here the body is white with black spots, like the Dalmatian dog.

Himalayan

Also two colours but a specific pattern of a basic white coat with either black or chocolate coloured ears, nose and feet.

Tricolour

The coat is made up of blocks of three different colours.

Tortoiseshell

Similar to tortoiseshell cats, these guinea pigs have red and black blocks of coloured hair. They can also be tricoloured with the addition of white and are then called tortoiseshell-and-white.

Coat type

Smooth

Known as English, American or Bolivian, the hair
is short, straight and smooth. This is the more
traditional type of guinea pig.

Satin

A fine silky coat with a shine to it.

Rough-coated

Known as Abyssinian. The hair is short and coarse and grows in swirls and ridges called rosettes or whorls.

- The American-crested has a single whorl on its forehead, sometimes, of a different colour to the rest of its body.

- The Teddy also has coarse, short hair which stands erect over the whole body.

- The Rex has no guard hairs, so the coat feels more springy and woolly.

Long-haired

Long haired guinea pigs require more care in that they need grooming every day. The hair can be so long that it is sometimes difficult to see the shape of the guinea pig underneath.

- Silkies or Shelties have long, straight hair.

- Peruvian have long, fine hair.

- Texels have long hair that grows in curls and ringlets.

Hairless

These guinea pigs cannot be kept outside as they do not have hair to protect them from the cold or from being sunburnt.

- The Skinny is hairless except for the head and lower legs.

- The Baldwin is born with hair but loses it all, becoming totally bald when it is about three weeks old.

The hairless Skinny guinea pig pictured

One guinea pig or two?

Guinea pigs are social animals and it is strongly recommended that you have two. This need to provide our guinea pigs with suitable company is part of our responsibility for caring for them. The best arrangement is to have a neutered male and one or more females. Two females can also live together and two neutered males, if they have been brought up together from birth (litter brothers).

Male guinea pigs can be neutered before they reach sexual maturity at 3- 4 months of age. Neutering will mean that you will not have unexpected baby guinea pigs which you may not be able to find good homes for. Neutering also helps prevent behaviour problems, such as fighting between males.

If you currently only have one guinea pig, you may wish to consider getting it a friend (of the opposite sex, and neutered if male). Most guinea pigs will greatly appreciate such company. Get your new guinea pig in the morning so they have all day to become acquainted. In the large run make sure there are several pipes and boxes so they can get away from each other if they wish, and put out lots of food, in several different parts of the run.

If your guinea pig has lived on its own for a long time it may not welcome another. In that case, you must make sure your guinea pig gets plenty of attention from you, every day. You may also wish to contact a good, reputable guinea pig rescue to see if they will be able to help find your guinea pig a friend and introduce them appropriately.

Guinea pigs & rabbits

It is not advised to keep guinea pigs and rabbits together for several reasons. First, although a single rabbit and guinea pig will provide some sort of company for each other, it will not be as good as having a member of their own kind.

In addition there are medical reasons why guinea pigs and rabbits may not be the best of cage mates. A rabbit may injure a guinea pig either by kicking it or attempting to mate it. In addition they have different dietary requirements for vitamin C, with guinea pigs needing additional supplements of this vitamin. Finally guinea pigs are at risk of developing a respiratory disease which is caused by a type of bacteria that is carried by rabbits and dogs.

Setting up home

Before you buy your guinea pigs, you will need to decide where you are going to keep them, and then get suitable housing.

Whether you keep them outside or in your home, the guinea pigs' accommodation must have both a hutch/ cage (safe sleeping area) and a permanently attached exercise area (run) that they can access when they want to. You may also have an additional run that you can move around the garden or safe areas where they can go free in your home. The hutch/ cage should be as large as possible and must enable the guinea-pigs to move freely and stand up fully on their back legs. It is recommended that the minimum size of the hutch/ cage is 6 feet x 2 feet x 2 feet high (1.8 m x 61 cm x 61 cm), the same as that recommended for a similar sized breed of rabbit. It should provide a dark and draught-free resting area.

The great outdoors

In temperate countries such as the UK, guinea pigs (except hairless ones) can live in an outside hutch-and-run complex all-year-round, as long as you take steps to make it as comfortable as possible for them.

- The hutch should be raised off the ground to prevent dampness and draughts.

- The hutch should have a separate sleeping compartment, with a cosy bed of paper topped with a deep bed of hay and straw.

The rest of the hutch should be lined with a thick layer of paper to absorb the guinea pigs' urine.

- Other appropriate bedding materials are products made from paper, corn cobs or hardwood. Do not use materials that are made from softwoods as these contain substances that can increase the risk of your guinea pig getting liver cancer.

Wood shavings and sawdust are not recommended as they can cause irritation to eyes, noses and lungs and dusty bedding can even lead to pneumonia.

- The living quarters should have a fine, wire-mesh front, to stop rats or mice getting in.

- Both the hutch and the run must be made secure to protect the guinea pigs from larger enemies such as cats and foxes.

- A water bottle for small animals and a hay rack should be fitted to the side of the hutch. Water bowls are not recommended as they can be spilt or get filled with bedding.

- The hutch and run must provide shelter from the prevailing wind and direct sunshine. Guinea pigs need somewhere cool and shady in hot weather as they are susceptible to overheating, and to having sunburnt ears!

In the winter, a hutch cover should be used. These can be bought or you can use some heavy sacking to reduce heat escaping from the roof of the hutch. This will provide extra protection from the cold. The cover can be pulled down over the front of the hutch at night, while still allowing sufficient fresh air. In cold weather, do ensure the guinea pigs' water has not frozen. Your guinea pigs need fresh drinking water at all times.

Outside run

Guinea pigs kept only in a hutch do not have very much room to move around, so they need a place where they can stretch their legs.

Ideally the run should be permanently attached to the hutch so they can have free access to it and choose to go out when they want to. If not, and you have to put your guinea pigs in the run, then make sure there is shelter. This should be a warm, dry, hay filled box, raised off the ground, and sheltered from the rain and wind. Ensure there is shade, perhaps by partially covering the run, then your guinea pigs can go out in the run in any weather, to enjoy the sun and snow! They should be given the opportunity to exercise for 6- 8 hours a day.

- The run should be as big as possible, with a shaded area at one end where the guinea pigs can go if it gets too hot or if it starts to rain.

- Attach a water-bottle to the side of the run. You should also provide a selection of vegetables for your guinea pigs to eat, and toys such as branches of (untreated) fruit trees that they can gnaw to help keep their teeth in tip-top condition.

If the run is on grass, remember to move it regularly so your guinea pigs have fresh grass to eat. Do not put the run on grass that has been treated with pesticides.

If the run is on concrete, provide an area filled with sand/ soil which will provide a soft resting place. A small sand pit is very suitable.

- The run should also contain things for your guinea pigs to use, and to help it feel safe, such as logs to sit on and use as look-out places, half pipes to run through or hide in, for example, when a large bird flies over the run or there is a loud noise.

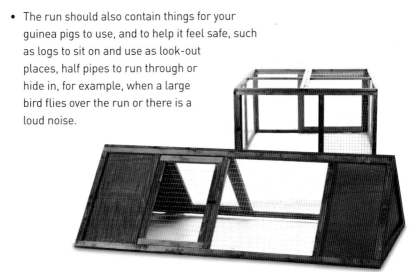

Indoor guinea pigs

Many owners like to keep their guinea pigs in the house. House guinea pigs need the same type of accommodation as those living outside, namely a hutch, or cage to use as a base and a run in which they can exercise daily.

A very important thing to be aware of is that guinea pigs do not tolerate heat and should be kept away from sunny windows and radiators and, of course draughts. Ideally the room temperature should be between 15– 22 degrees centigrade; unless your guinea pigs are hairless in which case they should be kept in temperatures no lower than 18 degrees centigrade.

Remember guinea pigs are highly sensitive to noise, and frightened of sudden noises, and should be kept in a quiet part of the house.

- The indoor cage should be as big as possible. You can buy specially-made cages, or you can adapt a rabbit cage. It will need to contain a dark, draught free sleeping area.

- The cage needs a shallow tray as a base which can be lined with paper and hay and straw just like an outside hutch.

- Attach a water bottle to the side of the cage.

- Ensure the cage and indoor run is safe from other pets, such as cats, dogs and snakes, and that the guinea pigs have places to hide if they feel scared.

Guinea pig proofing your home

You can use a large playpen so that your guinea pigs can exercise outside the cage, or you may prefer to guinea pig proof a room, where they can live and exercise in safety. You will need to watch out for the following hazards:

- Trailing electric wires.

- Floor-length curtains that are likely to be chewed.

- Houseplants will be seen as a tasty snack and are often poisonous.

- Furniture, especially legs of wooden tables and chairs which your guinea pigs can chew. Do supervise your guinea pigs, especially if you have dogs or cats, ferrets or snakes.

Playtime

Guinea pigs, whether they are kept in the house or outside, should be given the chance to behave naturally. They are social and inquisitive animals and in the wild would tunnel through the long grass, play, socialise and forage for food. Guinea pigs must eat plenty of grass or hay to keep their teeth and digestive system in good order.

All guinea pigs should be given appropriate toys to play with, lots of hay, and you may even wish to teach them tricks.

Teaching tricks can be a great way of bonding with your guinea pigs and is lots of fun (see Sources of further information p126). They can be taught to come when called, go back to their cage on cue, even retrieve small objects.

You can help your guinea pigs to live a full life by doing the following:

- Give them plenty of hay every day. Give them toys made of natural, untreated wood, such as willow, or wooden toys made for parrots. Do not give hard, plastic toys. If a guinea pig swallows a fragment it may become extremely ill.

- Create hiding places from tunnels or a cardboard box filled with hay and a hole cut in the side. You can scatter this with some fresh herbs, or pellet guinea pig food. This gives your pets the chance to rummage among the hay for some tasty treats and chew up the cardboard box, lots of guinea pig fun! A similar idea is to stuff the cardboard centres of toilet rolls with hay.

Sourcing your guinea pigs

There should be a wide variety of guinea pigs available at your local pet store, kept in spacious runs so you will have the opportunity to watch them and make your choice.

You could consider giving unwanted guinea pigs a new home. Many pet stores now have adoption centres and of course there are many associations that are constantly looking to re-home unwanted pets.

If you are interested in a particular breed, then you may wish to get your guinea pig from a reputable breeder.

Signs of a healthy guinea pig

Check that the guinea pigs you choose are fit and well.

Mouth

There should be no signs of dribbling, which could mean the teeth are overgrown.

Eyes

Look for bright, clear eyes, with no discharge.

Ears

Check the inside of the ears to see if they look and smell clean. There should be no sign of damage on the outer ear.

Coat

The coat should be clean and glossy, with no scurf, dandruff or bald patches.

Body

The body should be rounded and plump looking, with no lumps or swellings.

Bottom

Check the rear for any matting or soiling, which could indicate diarrhoea, and is a sign that your guinea pig may have teeth or intestine problems, or is too fat, or being fed the wrong diet.

Breathing

Watching and listening to the guinea pig's chest will enable you to check its breathing, which should be quiet and regular.

Movement

Look for free movement; there should be no sign of lameness.

Making friends

Though guinea pigs are naturally friendly and sociable animals, they are easily frightened and will be anxious when they first come to their new home with you. If you spend time getting to know your guinea pigs, they will stop being frightened of you and become very tame.

When you first bring them home, you will want to stroke and play with them, but you must be patient. For the first couple of days, your guinea pigs need peace and quiet to settle into their new home. You will need to provide food, and change the water, so they will start getting used to you, without the stress of being handled. You can even train them to come to you when you whistle softy before you put the food down. They will soon learn that your whistle means something pleasant.

Handling

When your guinea pigs appear to be happy and relaxed, you can start making friends.

- To begin with, come close to the hutch or cage, and talk to them. Do not make any sudden movements which will alarm them.

- Offer treats so the guinea pigs have to come up to see you, and get used to your hand.

- Now try stroking your guinea pig, just before you give it a treat. Most love to have their heads gently stroked just behind the ears. Just use one finger to begin with, and gently stroke their backs while they are eating.

- Only when they are calm and relaxed should you start to use your whole hand to stroke them.

The next stage is to get the guinea pig out of the hutch or cage. Be very careful as a guinea pig will panic easily. Like all prey species, guinea pigs can find being picked up and carried around very scary.

Use one hand to slide under the guinea pig, so that a couple of fingers support its collarbone, the rest of your fingers support its chest and your thumb wraps around its shoulder. The other hand should be cupped under its rump, fully supporting its weight. Then bring it up to rest against your chest. When picking up or holding your guinea pig, always use a firm but gentle grasp around its shoulder with one hand, and put the other under its rump so you are fully supporting its weight.

As soon as you have it out of the hutch, hold it gently on your lap while you sit on the floor. In this way it is less likely to be injured if it should wriggle. Never pass a guinea pig to a child while you are standing, as the height and motion of being passed from one person to another can be very frightening and cause it to panic. It would be a bit like you being passed from the top of one skyscraper to another! A frightened guinea pig can move very fast and will wriggle and potentially get dropped or be squeezed too hard as you, or the child, try to hold it still. Squeezing can cause damage to the internal organs, even rupturing the guinea pig's liver.

Guinea pigs will enjoy being gently stroked while sitting on your lap and will often purr in contentment. They will also let you know when they have had enough by rubbing your hand with their teeth. If that is not heeded they may nip to get the message across.

Do not turn your guinea pig on its back and stroke its tummy. It will lie very still, because this is a very scary position for him – he is playing dead to deter a predator. He will remain like this until he thinks the danger has passed. This is a common behaviour in many small animals. Do not be fooled into thinking that he is relaxed or in a trance. Research has shown that he is very alert and stressed. When he thinks it is safe to do so he will suddenly kick out to 'escape' and may get injured.

Other pets

If you have other pets, such as a dog, cat or ferret you will need to be very careful, especially if you are keeping guinea pigs in the house or allowing them free access to areas where other pets are around.

To start with, the dog should meet the guinea pigs when they are safely in the hutch or cage. The guinea pigs will feel frightened, so keep the dog at a distance. Reward the dog with a tasty treat if it remains calm and well behaved. Repeat this exercise many times until the dog loses interest in the guinea pigs. But, remember, you should never allow other pets near without supervision. Dog, cats, ferrets and snakes are meat-eaters and you would not want your guinea pig to end up as their snack.

Food glorious food

A well-balanced diet will keep your guinea pigs healthy, and will help to ensure a good, long life.

In the wild, guinea pigs eat grass and plants and graze throughout the day. It is essential that they eat a lot of grass or hay, which are high in fibre, and fresh vegetables. This stops their teeth growing too long, and ensures their digestion is working. If not, they can quickly suffer from gut stasis, where the guts no longer work, and die. Lack of hay and fresh vegetables can mean your guinea pigs develop serious and painful dental problems or suffer from a lack of vitamin C.

It is very important not to over-feed, particularly if your guinea pigs live in the house. Guinea pigs living outside need more food to give them the energy to stay warm. Those in the house do not need to do this, and will easily become overweight.

Hay

Guinea pigs need a high level of fibre in their diet, and this is supplied by eating hay or grass. Dried grass is available, but hay is usually easier to obtain. Make sure you buy good-quality hay that smells sweet, meadow hay is ideal. Do not feed hay that is dusty or mouldy.

Hay should be available to your guinea pigs at all times, and should be the main part of their diet.

Vegetables

Guinea pigs love and need fresh vegetables. Like humans, guinea pigs have to have a supply of vitamin C in their diet; otherwise they will develop hypovitaminosis C, also known as Scurvy, which is a very painful and even fatal condition. Humans and guinea pigs, unlike other animals cannot make their own vitamin C. They must be given a supply, and the best way is fresh fruit and vegetables. However, do not give them citrus fruit, such as oranges, as these can cause painful inflammation of your guinea pigs lips. Likewise, green vegetables are better than fruit or starchy vegetables, as these can lead to bloat.

Guinea pigs favourites include clover and sorrel, dandelion leaves, groundsel, chickweed and watercress. Excellent sources of fibre and vitamin C are broccoli, cabbage, kale, celery, cucumber, sweetcorn, green beans. These can be given daily. On occasion and only in moderation, carrots, apples, banana, tomatoes, pear, melon and kiwi fruit will be much appreciated special additions to their dinner.

Avoid onions, leeks, garlic, or anything else grown from a bulb and do not feed rhubarb or raw potatoes. Do not feed grass cuttings from a lawn mower, give hand picked grass only.

When giving any fresh food to your pet it is important to make sure it is rinsed well under cold water to clean away any dirt or insects. You should never feed any fruit or vegetable that is over or under-ripe or that is wilting, as this is not healthy for your guinea pigs. A good rule of thumb to follow is: would you eat it? If not then do not feed it to your pet.

Never collect fresh plants from the side of the road or from areas that have been, or are likely to have been, sprayed with pesticides, as this is harmful to your guinea pigs. Instead, try to grow your own fresh herbs and vegetables for your pets. Not only will they taste fresh and crisp but it will also be great fun for your children or yourself to grow the treats for your pets.

Complementary diets

Supplementary feeding

While grass, hay and fresh vegetables are extremely important and should make up the bulk of your guinea pigs' diet, they also need supplements in order to ensure they have enough of essential nutrients like vitamin C. There are a number of diets that are specially made for guinea pigs, which contain the nutrients needed to keep them healthy. These are available from your local pet store and are either in the form of pellets or mixes that resemble human muesli breakfast cereals. Because guinea pigs are naturally 'fussy' eaters, known as selective feeders, pellet diets are better than muesli types, as they will tend to leave the bits they do not much like, even though they need to eat it all to get all the nutrients. However, whichever type you choose, these should not form the bulk of their diet. Overfeeding of such diets can lead to problems with the guinea pigs' teeth and intestines, obesity and boredom. As a rough guide, an egg cupful of pellet diet is appropriate for each animal, however, how much an animal needs to eat will depend on its age, lifestyle and health, so do ask your vet if you have any queries. If a guinea pig eats more food than it needs it will get fat and may suffer.

Because vitamin C degrades very quickly, commercial diets must be used before the best before date.

Vitamin C supplements

Vitamin C is so important to your guinea pig's diet – If you are not sure your pet is getting enough, there are supplementary sources produced by some pet food manufacturers that you can add to your pets' daily food. You could even use a 50 mg human vitamin C chew tablet crumbled on the food daily (only vitamin C, not a multivitamin). Do not give vitamin C in water as it deteriorates very quickly and will not help your pet.

How much?

Guinea pigs are grazers, so they eat throughout the day and night. Hay should always be available for them. Vegetables and their ration of commercial diet can be given once a day or split over two feeding times.

As a rough guide 70% of their diet should be hay, 20% fresh vegetables and only 10% pellet or muesli type guinea pig food.

Guinea pig care

Looking after guinea pigs means you need to keep their house clean and watch out for health problems. Cleaning out a cage or hutch might not be the most fun aspect of owning guinea pigs, but it is very rewarding when you think that you are making them as clean and comfortable as possible.

Daily tasks

Find time every day to do the following:

- Remove all uneaten food, and wash the feed bowls. If you frequently find uneaten food in the bowls, it means you are feeding too much, so give them less next time.

- Refill the water-bottle with fresh water.

- Refill the hayrack with fresh hay.

- Remove wet bedding and droppings.

- Give your guinea pigs access to the exercise run for several hours a day.

- Check your guinea pig's bottom to ensure it is clean. See the 'Health' section for more information on daily checks.

Weekly tasks

Once a week you will need to confine
your guinea pigs to the exercise area
so you can clean the cage or hutch
thoroughly.

- Remove all bedding and clean out the cage or
  hutch with an 'animal friendly' disinfectant.

- Clean the water bottle.

- Replace all bedding material.

- Check your guinea pigs' teeth and run your fingers
  gently along the jaw line to check for any bumps.

- Check your guinea pigs' nails.

- Groom them and check for mites or any other
  problems such as lumps or wounds.

- Check your guinea pigs are not getting fat.

Grooming

The amount of grooming each guinea pig needs depends on coat length. All guinea pigs should be brushed weekly, even short-haired ones.

However, long haired guinea pigs will need to be groomed ideally every day or every other day, to prevent mats and tangles. Grooming helps keep the coat and underlying skin healthy. It also enables you to check for any problems. A baby's toothbrush makes an ideal brush for your guinea pig. If your guinea pig has long hair, ensure you hold the hair below the knot and gently tug with small flicks of the brush. Do not tug or pull too hard or you may pull the hair out from the skin or even tear the skin. If the knot or tangle is not being moved easily, cut it away with a pair of curved surgical scissors.

Start grooming from an early age, perhaps when the guinea pig is enjoying some tasty vegetables, so that it learns to relax and enjoy the attention.

Nails

In the wild, a guinea pig would keep its nails in trim by running on soil and across stones. A pet guinea pig's nails may grow too long, which will make moving very uncomfortable as they can curve over and dig into the bottom of the feet.

Placing some rougher surfaces in your guinea pigs' home can help keep their nails in good condition. A simple way is to put a few bricks down to make a platform big enough for them to walk on, or a couple of concrete paving stones. Putting their vegetables on this means they will have to climb and walk on the rough surface, which will help wear the nails.

Nails can be clipped with nail-clippers used for cats, but you will need to ask a vet or an experienced guinea pig keeper to do this for you, or show you how to do it, as you must be careful not to cut an adjacent toe or cut the nail too short to the quick or nail-bed. The nail bed is pink coloured as it contains blood vessels, and nerves. While easy to see on light coloured nails, if your guinea pig has dark nails it can be difficult to judge where the quick is. In that case, trim the nails to the same length as any white ones your guinea pig has, or just remove the tip.

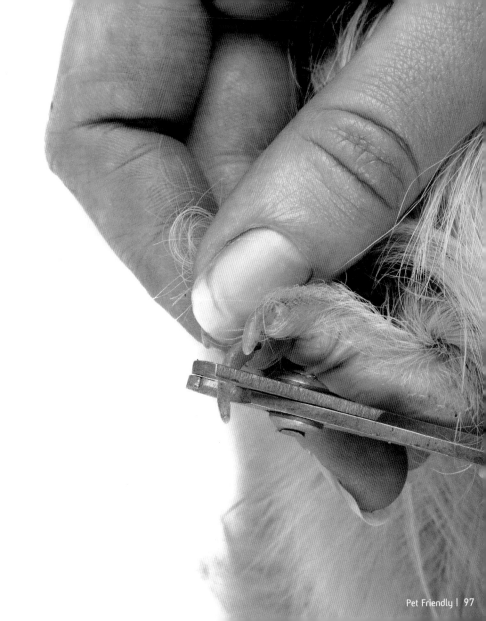

Cutting the nail-bed is very painful and will probably bleed. If this happens, apply some pressure for a few minutes until the bleeding stops. Alternatively, dip the toe into some wound powder made specifically for small animals, or put a blob of Vaseline or flour on the end of the wounded nail to seal it.

Bathing

You should only bathe your guinea pig on a very occasionally basis; it is likely to be a stressful rather than a pleasant experience for your pet. If you groom your pet regularly there is less need to bathe him. Sometimes owners like to bathe their guinea pig to get rid of any staining on the coat, particularly on the longer haired varieties. Bathing can also be useful in getting rid of mites.

To bathe your pet you will need a bowl with a non-slip surface so your guinea pig will feel safe. A plastic washing up bowl is suitable. You will also need a soft towel, some small animal shampoo, available from your pet shop, a small plastic cup and a bowl of clean tepid water to use to rinse your pet. A hair drier can be useful when drying your guinea pig after its bath. Put a couple of inches of tepid water in the bowl. Remember not to make the water hot; what you may feel is warm may be too hot for your guinea pig.

Gently put your guinea pig in the water and shield its face and eyes with one hand, whilst you scoop water with your other hand or the plastic cup, over the body starting at the rump, and slowly moving towards the head, gently talking to your pet all the while. Remember not to move suddenly as this will frighten your pet.

Once the coat is wet, gently massage in a small amount of the shampoo, but avoid the head, eyes and ears! Then you will need to rinse your pet's coat using the water in which it is standing and a final rinse or two with the clean water from the other bowl. Follow the same method as when you started to wet the coat and rinse clean, so all the soap suds have gone and the water runs clear from the coat.

You now need to dry your guinea pig. Sit on the floor with your guinea pig on your lap so if it gets frightened by the hair drier it will not injure itself if it runs away. Gently rub the coat with the soft towel until it is just moist and then use the hair drier, on its low setting and held 12 inches away, to blow the hair almost dry. Be careful not to burn your pet. Keep moving the hair drier across the coat. Do not dry the hair completely, again to avoid burns, but let it finish off naturally. For this you need to keep your pet indoors in the warm as having wet hair outside may cause it to catch a chill, even on a warm day.

Teeth

Keep a close check on your guinea pigs' teeth
to make sure they do not grow too long or are
misaligned. This can indicate a variety of possible
problems including inadequate diet, fractured
teeth from a fall, abscesses or some other illness.
If your guinea pig is drooling, or having difficulty
eating, you need to take your guinea pig to the vet.
Be warned, overgrown teeth can lead to serious
and even fatal problems for guinea pigs. The
chance of your guinea pig developing
teeth problems is greatly
reduced if they have
lots of hay and
vegetables to eat.

Guinea pig behaviour

One of the most rewarding things about owning a pet is learning to understand what it is thinking or feeling. If you have two or more guinea pigs, you will witness their natural behaviour as they interact with each other. You can also learn a lot about what your guinea pigs are saying to you, and to each other by listening to the sounds they make and observing their body postures.

Listen to your guinea pigs.

Guinea pigs are very chatty animals, and this is one of the things that makes them such attractive pets. They have at least 11 different types of sound.

Sounds of a happy guinea pig

Chutt/ putt

This is a short sound that guinea pigs use when they are exploring something new.

Cooing

This is a sound of contentment. Mother guinea pigs coo to their babies, and guinea pigs will sometimes coo to their owners.

Purring/ bubbling/ chortling

A sign of a relaxed guinea pig, this is made when seeking or enjoying physical contact such as being stroked by you or groomed by another guinea pig.

Wheek/ whistle

This sound is made by a guinea pig who is excited. They will make this noise when they hear you coming with their food. It can also be made when they are trying to locate other guinea pigs when they are separated.

Rumblestrutting

A high pitched vibration sound made by a male guinea pig trying to woo a female. It is accompanied by him wiggling his hindquarters – his courtship dance.

Sounds of a stressed/ frightened guinea pig

Rumbling/ motor boating

A low vibrating sound, a bit like a motorboat or growl, this is made by an animal that is scared or wanting to be left alone.

Chattering

This is a warning signal made by gnashing the teeth together rapidly. It is made to tell other guinea pigs, or people, to stay away. It can also be a sign of frustration.

Chirping

This sounds rather like a bird chirp and is indicative of stress. In young guinea pigs it tells the mother that they are hungry and want to suckle from her.

Squeak

This high-pitched noise is made by a guinea pig who is frightened or in pain. Sometimes young guinea pigs will make this sound when they are taken away from their mother or are alone.

Watch your guinea pigs

Scent rubbing

Scent is an important part of guinea pig communication, though we cannot detect it. You will see your guinea pig drag its bottom on the ground to leave a scent trail. It will also rub its chin or cheeks on new objects in his territory to claim them as his own. Sometimes you may see guinea pigs mark each other with urine. Males do this to females as part of their courtship. Females urine spray males to deter them.

When meeting a new individual, guinea pigs will smell each other under the chin and around the bottom. Friendly greetings are face to face, whisker to whisker.

Relaxed & happy guinea pigs

Popcorning

Used in play, this is when the guinea pig leaps in the air from a standstill, with all four feet off the ground, often changing direction in mid jump.

However popcorning is also used when guinea pigs are very frightened and running away from something such as a predator. The movement is intended to confuse the predator and help the guinea pig escape to safety. This flight is sometimes called stampeding as the guinea pigs run all over the place in a panic. They can easily injure themselves in this state, for example, by falling off a table. This is why it is important to keep your guinea pigs on the ground when you are playing with them.

Nose to tail

A bit like playing trains, guinea pigs will follow each other.

Lying stretched out

A relaxed, contented guinea pig will stretch out on its side or tummy.

Sitting/ lying in contact with another

Guinea pigs are social animals and like to be near each other.

Grooming another guinea pig

Grooming each other is a sign of attachment between guinea pigs. However, this should not cause any hair loss and if you see any baldness, particularly in the shoulder area, it may indicate over grooming or 'barbering' and can mean that your guinea pigs are stressed.

Annoyed guinea pigs

Stiff legged trotting is usually a male behaviour and is a ritual display to see who the boss is. It is often accompanied by standing face to face and jabbing their heads at each other. Such displays will rarely end in biting, unless there is not enough space or things for them to do, in which case aggression may be seen in the group.

Guinea pigs, of either sex, who stand upright on their back legs, with no support, are saying they are prepared to fight.

Frightened guinea pigs

Freezing

When a guinea pig suddenly stops what it is doing and 'freezes on the spot' it means it has heard, seen or smelt something unusual and scary. It is frightened. This is usually followed by the guinea pig running back to a safe shelter.

Playing Dead

If your guinea pig lies absolutely still, usually on its back, it is extremely frightened. It is trying to pretend to be dead and thus of no interest to a predator. It will remain like this until the scary thing has gone away. This is a common behaviour in many small animals, including rabbits. Do not be fooled and think your guinea pig is in a trance or is relaxed. Research has shown that they are very alert and stressed.

Health

Health

Guinea pigs can live up 6- 8 years, but sadly many do not reach old age. This short life is usually due to owners not understanding the guinea pigs' needs and providing a poor diet and inadequate accommodation.

Handling your pet every day and performing regular health checks will help you pick up on the early signs of ill health and take action quickly to treat ailments before they become too serious. This is best done while handling your pet in the normal way. You should do any examinations as part of your grooming and regular play.

Weigh your guinea pigs on a regular basis and remember to keep a record of their weight. Weight loss is often the first sign of ill health in guinea pigs.

You should know how your pet behaves while healthy. A sudden change in their normal pattern of behaviour can also indicate ill health, such as change in their eating habits, hiding more, or becoming aggressive.

Guinea pigs are very good at disguising signs of illness and pain, so familiarity with your own pets is vital. As a guide, signs of a poorly guinea pig can include a greasy coat, hunched body, faded and dull eyes and loose stools. It is important that you contact a vet as soon as possible if you have any concerns about your guinea pig's health.

The sick bed

It is prudent to have a spare cage available if you have a sick guinea pig. Keep them in sight of his cage friend to prevent stress unless you are told otherwise by your vet.

If you think your guinea pig is unwell, you must seek veterinary help. Signs such as diarrhoea, a swollen tummy or a lack of interest in food, can all indicate problems that can quickly become fatal, even within a day.

Take your guinea pig to the vet in a secure box, lined with some soft bedding, and with air holes in the top and sides, or you can buy an appropriate sized travel box for your pet.

Illness & injuries

Accidents, injuries or illness may happen and in the first instance a vet should be contacted to arrange treatment. But, in the time between the discovery of a problem and reaching the vet surgery you are responsible for providing the best care you can.

Mishaps

Because guinea pigs are so easily frightened they may be dropped or hurt when trying to run away from something that has scared them. They have very fine bones which can easily fracture. If you believe your pet has suffered a broken or fractured bone, phone your vet immediately. Your vet may advise you to bring your pet in as soon as possible for stabilisation and pain relief. In the meantime keep in a darkened and quiet area. He will feel more safe and relaxed in a dark enclosed space, such as his travelling box lined with soft bedding.

Wounds

It is possible that your guinea pig will cut himself as he is playing. He may even get bitten, though if there are lots of things for your animals to do and plenty of space and hiding places this will be very rare. If you do see bite wounds then ask your vet for behaviour advice.

Most minor injuries can be simply treated by being cleaned, using a cotton bud, with salty water (tap water and rock salt). However, more serious injuries and bites must be looked at and treated by a veterinary surgeon as soon as possible to prevent infection and abscesses. Try and keep the wound as clean as possible until you go to the vet.

Constipation & diarrhoea

These conditions should be taken very seriously as they can have a number of causes and can rapidly be fatal. Both can be caused by a poor diet, pain or an illness. It may also mean that your guinea pig has eaten something poisonous, such as a houseplant. Guinea pigs cannot vomit when they feel sick, everything they eat has to go through the whole gut. Consult a vet for advice and treatment as soon as you can.

Parasites

Scratching and/ or hair loss are common symptoms of skin complaints brought about by parasites such as lice, mites and mange or fungal infections like ringworm. These can occur if your guinea pigs have been stressed, or can be passed on from other animals. Some, like ringworm can affect people too. Treatment may involve a specialised medicated shampoo, mild insecticide powder or small animal spot-on preparation. Do not use treatments designed for dogs and cats as these can be fatal to guinea pigs. Hair loss in older female guinea pigs may indicate ovarian cysts.

Respiratory infections

Guinea pigs are prone to chest infections and if left untreated these can develop into pneumonia and be fatal. Animals that recover may still carry the bacteria and pass the illness on to other guinea pigs. Guinea pigs can also catch the illness from rabbits and young puppies, which can carry the bacteria but may not be ill themselves. Guinea pigs are more prone to illness if they are in a damp environment, overcrowded, and are not kept in clean conditions and fed correctly.

Note that guinea pigs with a discharge from their eyes may have conjunctivitis and while they may recover with no treatment, it can progress to bronchitis or pneumonia, so do get your pet checked by the vet.

Teeth

Unfortunately, dental disease is common in guinea pigs. Guinea pig teeth grow continuously throughout their lives, both the front incisor teeth and the molars at the back of the mouth. They must be worn down by eating hay, grass and fresh vegetables. Teeth that are overgrown can prevent the guinea pig eating properly and may be very painful. Overgrown molars can cause the tongue and cheeks to be torn. In fact problems with the front teeth are often a later sign of molar problems.

Teeth problems can be due to too little fibre or vitamin C in the diet, fractures from being dropped, or the guinea pig catching its front teeth in the wire mesh of the cage. Stress, such as changes in the environment or too much noise, can also mean guinea pigs do not eat well and lead to dental problems.

If you notice your guinea pig has a wet chin, is drooling, not eating as much or losing weight, take it to the veterinary surgeon.

Vitamin C deficiency

This can cause teeth, bone and skin problems. It can even be the underlying cause in your guinea pig becoming paralysed, as the bones are weakened and more likely to fracture. Lack of vitamin C can cause your guinea pig to find it painful to breathe because of rib lesions. It is easily prevented by ensuring the diet you feed your pet is adequate.

Urinary tract disease

Male and female guinea pigs can suffer from cystitis and it is quite common, though not easily detected until it is quite advanced. Guinea pigs with severe cystitis will be in pain and may even scream when urinating. Again a good diet will help prevent this problem.

Bumble foot

This is an extremely painful condition. It is characterised by the feet being swollen and displaying pus-filled scabs. The infection can spread to the bones of the feet and, if you see such signs on the feet of your guinea pig, then you must take it to the vet as soon as possible.

A major cause of bumble foot is keeping guinea pigs on mesh floors rather than flat floors. They should have a thick layer of paper on the floor of their home, to provide a flat, insulated surface and hay or straw on the top for them to burrow and snuggle in. Do not use wood shavings or sawdust as these can cause irritations to the eyes and the dust can lead to lung infections and pneumonia.

Head tilt

This is caused by a middle ear infection, otitis media. It can progress quite slowly and can be unnoticeable until the guinea pig has developed a tilt, holding its head to one side. In severe cases it may start to fall over to one side as its balance is affected. Take your guinea pig to the vet to get a diagnosis, in case there is some other cause. There is no cure for Otitis media, but many guinea pigs with a tilt can cope quite well, and continue to enjoy life.

Guinea pig medicine

Veterinary knowledge of guinea pigs has increased hugely over the last few years and now there is much more that can be done to treat your pet. However, unlike cat and dog medicine which all veterinary surgeons know a lot about, guinea pigs like other small animals are a specialist subject and it is worth finding a vet who is interested in guinea pigs and their treatment.

Know your guinea pig

Scientific name	Cavia aperea f. porcellus
Group order	Rodentia
Breeding age	Males 3- 4 months; Females 2- 3 months
Gestation	59- 72 days
Litter size	1- 6 (average 3- 4)
Birth weight	60- 100 g approx
Birth type	Fully furred, mobile
Eyes open	At birth
Weaning	2- 3 weeks
Adult weight	500- 900 g (1- 2 lbs), males are larger than females.

Sources of further information

Orr, J and Lewin, T 2005 Getting Started: clicking with your rabbit. Karen Pryor Publications. Gives excellent advice on how to train rabbits, which can also be applied to guinea pigs.

Richardson, V 1999 Rabbit Nutrition Coney Publications an illustrated guide to plants and vegetables, wild and cultivated that can be fed to your rabbit and guinea pig.

Websites

www.clickerbunny.com/clickercritterarticles.html

www.nationalcavyclub.co.uk – Provides information on guinea pigs, their care, breeding and showing.

www.cavyclub.co.uk – the UK Pet Cavy Club is a forum for owners of pet guinea pigs.

www.rspcaorg.uk – guinea pig care advice. Produced by the RSPCA this gives advice on how to care for and meet your legal responsibilities to your guinea pig under the UK Animal Welfare Act (2006).

Weights & measures

If you prefer your units in pounds and inches, you can use this conversion chart:

Length in inches	Length in cm	Weight in kg	Weight in lb
1	2.5	0.5	1.1
2	5.1	0.7	1.5
3	7.6	1	2.2
4	10.2	1.5	3.3
5	12.7	2	4.4
8	20.3	3	6.6
10	25.4	4	8.8
15	38.1	5	11

Measurements rounded to 1 decimal place.